THE PRENUPTIAL, POSTNUPTIAL, & COHABITATION AGREEMENTS

TEXAS HANDBOOK

BRYAN JOSEPH FAGAN

For additional information contact:

Bryan Fagan

Law Office of Bryan Fagan

3707 Cypress Creek Pkwy Suite 400

Houston, TX 77068

Tel: (832) 219-6692

Fax: (855) 668-0536

www.bryanfagan.com

FIRST EDITION

ISBN-13: 978-1-7328903-1-2 (Law Office of Bryan Fagan) Legal Disclaimer:
This Book is Not Legal Advice.

While this book provides a good amount of legal information, the intent is that it is to be used strictly for review and educational purposes only. This information is in no way intended to be interpreted as legal advice about any particular situation. You should seek the advice of an attorney before acting on any of the information provided. There is no substitute for legal advice from a qualified, licensed attorney.

The material in this book may be considered advertising under applicable rules.

FOREWORD

"To be fully seen by somebody, then, and be loved anyhow–this is a human offering that can border on miraculous." – Elizabeth Gilbert

The Prenuptial, Postnuptial, & Cohabitation Agreements Texas Handbook is a guide to help you start asking the right questions. Many of the myths, misconceptions and frequently asked questions regarding prenuptial and postnuptial agreements are also tackled. Use it accordingly: mark it up, fold down the pages, highlight important topics, make notes in the margins and pass it along to a friend in need. Use it as it was intended to be used...as a guide for those in search of answers.

Do NOT, however, allow this book to take the place of consulting an actual Texas Family Law Attorney and sharing the specific facts and circumstances of your situation. Nothing can take the place of a live consultation with a knowledgeable attorney.

Therefore, I'm offering a free consultation with an attorney at my law !rm, a $500 value, to encourage you to find the answers you need to navigate toward a successful future.

Call our office today:
(832) 219-6692
www.bryanfagan.com

Call to make your appointment for a FREE 60-MINUTE consultation today
– A $500 Value –

INTRODUCTION

After years of serving as a divorce and family law attorney I have come to believe that many of the arguments that lead a couple to !le for divorce, or the more unpleasant divorces, could have been avoided if some planning or discussions had taken place before the marriage.

As with my first two books, this book is an aggregated, curated, and updated version of some of my most popular blog posts from the past few years. If you are reading my book, you are probably interested in how you and your future or current spouse can create your own rules for the marriage.

If you think about it, most of us are planning all the time for things we do not want to have happen. We purchase car insurance, life insurance, homeowner's insurance. Some even have our cell phones insured. The hope is, of course, that this insurance protection will never be needed, but we still get it just in case, because we know bad things can happen, even when we have nothing but the best of intentions.

In many ways, premarital agreements (prenuptial agreements) and postnuptial agreements (partition and exchange agreements) can be seen as simply another in the long list of insurance policies you may choose to put in place. In the case of the agreements, you are "insuring" the decisions about money and property issues related to your marriage, in the event there is a divorce.

In writing this book for you, I made it my goal to explain many practical reasons a premarital agreement may be needed and the types of things it can cover. This book was written for:

1. couples with children from previous marriages
2. couples with extreme differences in income levels
3. couples in which one spouse is part of a family business
4. couples planning for one spouse to stay at home and raise the children
5. couples in which one spouse has a professional practice
6. couples where one spouse has medical issues or is disabled

Really, any couple with financial or property issues at stake should learn how a premarital agreement could benefit them. What happens if you and your fiancé decide not to marry, but you still want to put some financial protections in place if your relationship comes to an end? In that case you will want to consider a cohabitation agreement. Under current Texas law these agreements are not enforceable unless they are in writing. It is important to get a lawyer's assistance if you are thinking of entering into such an agreement.

Indeed, discussing a premarital agreement with your fiancé or discussing a postmarital agreement after your wedding may feel unromantic. However, at the same time, getting on the same page regarding essential topics can make your relationship more robust and more romantic.

Having helped several people through divorce, I can say with confidence that communication or the lack thereof about money is one of the biggest stressors in a relationship. From my perspective couples who can communicate clearly and openly with each other about their finances and their expectations for the future are generally in a better position to protect their marriage.

I believe that working with an experienced attorney to establish a premarital agreement can accomplish a framework to discuss sensitive issues for a couple. When handled properly, a premarital agreement can be what author Steven Covey calls "win-win."

My hope is that this guide can empower you and help you feel more in control of your future. Our legal team here at the Law Office of Bryan Fagan has drawn from our vast legal experience to give you real life examples, important tips, and understandable explanations of current Texas law concerning these agreements.

Your situation is unique and as such so will be your legal needs. Marital agreements are not a one size #ts all situation. Please understand our guide is not a substitute for personal legal advice. If you are considering a Texas premarital agreement or postmarital agreement we can help you. If you have any questions after reading our guide and wish to discuss the specifics of your situation, please contact us to set up a free consultation. We are here whenever you need us.

CHAPTER 1
WHAT IS A PRENUPTIAL AGREEMENT IN TEXAS?

BEFORE WE TALK about prenuptial agreements, we should start with what a prenuptial agreement is. According to Black's Legal Dictionary, a prenuptial agreement is:

A written contract between two people who are about to marry, setting out terms of possession of assets, treatment of future earnings, control of the property of each, and potential division if marriage is later dissolved. These agreements are fairly common if either or both parties have substantial assets, children from a prior marriage, potential inheritances, high incomes, or have been "taken" by a previous spouse.

The word "prenuptial" refers to the premarital status of two individuals preparing to marry each other. The Texas Family Code refers to these agreements as "premarital agreements" and not "prenuptial agreements."

You can also find them mentioned in Texas case law as:

1. Prenuptial
2. premarital or
3. ante-nuptial agreements ("prenups").

They are governed in Texas by Texas Family Code Chapter 4. A prenuptial agreement is only possible when made between prospective spouses in contemplation of their marriage. Getting married is a material condition! The Texas Family Code Section 4.004 says that premarital agreements are effective upon marriage, but not before.

SIMILAR TYPES OF AGREEMENTS

Couples who are already married can draw up a similar agreement known as a postnuptial agreement. Under the family code, it is referred to as a Partition and Exchange Agreement.

Couples living together and not married but who would like the benefits of a prenuptial agreement can make such arrangements by entering a cohabitation agreement.

WEDDING POSTPONED

Many questions may arise that were not originally contemplated when the agreement was drafted. For example:

1. What happens when the wedding is postponed after the contract was signed?
2. What if the wedding is called o" permanently?

In such cases, to be sure, the couple may want to ratify their agreement in writing to revive it and ensure enforceability. If the wedding is called o" permanently, the prenup is unenforceable.

A similar agreement is known as a postnuptial agreement (or postmarital contract), which handles identical issues between couples after they are married. A postnuptial agreement has its origins in a prenuptial agreement.

PRENUPTIAL AGREEMENTS ARE NOT A NEW INVENTION

Prenuptial agreements are not a new legal invention. Marriage contracts have been around for centuries. However, in the United States, most courts in this country held that "contracts intended to facilitate or promote the procurement of a divorce will be declared illegal as contrary to public policy." That perspective began to change with the Florida Supreme Court's landmark decision in Mr. and Mrs. Posner's divorce *Posner, 233 So2d 381 (Fla. 1970).*

The Posner court held the opposite was true, that antenuptial agreements (or prenups) promote the public policy of encouraging marriage. Prenuptial agreements do this by settling property and alimony issues prior to a wedding taking place. This is especially true in cases where there is wealth disparity between the couples. Without a prenup, a marriage of economic extremes may be less likely to take place.

Although it took almost two decades, Texas adopted a version of the Uniform Premarital Agreement Act, and it became law in this state in 1987. The Statute is found under chapter 4 of the Texas Family Code Sections 4.001-4.010.

Drafting a prenup to withstand legal challenges when it matters upon divorce or a spouse's death is not a do-it-yourself project. In the event of a divorce, some agreements specify:

1. the rights and obligations of each of the parties regarding any of the property of either or both of them whenever and wherever acquired or located;
2. the right to buy, sell, use, transfer, exchange, abandon, lease, consume, expend, assign, create a security interest in, mortgage, encumber, dispose of, or otherwise manage and control property;
3. the disposition of property on separation, marital dissolution, death, or the occurrence or nonoccurrence of any other event;

4. the modification or elimination of spousal support;
5. the making of a will, trust, or other arrangement to carry out the provisions of the agreement;
6. the ownership rights in and disposition of the death benefit from a life insurance policy;
7. the choice of law governing the construction of the agreement; and
8. any other matter, including their personal rights and obligations, not in violation of public policy or a statute imposing a criminal penalty.

The right of a child to support may not be adversely affected by a premarital agreement.

Understand that Texas law is intended to encourage marriage generally, to unify expectations, and help the relationship work more smoothly. Given roughly half of first marriages and more than 60% of all second marriages end in divorce, having a prenuptial agreement can ease marital dissolution's financial complexities by making divorce proceedings significantly less arduous, both emotionally and financially. The same can be said of prenuptial agreements in probate proceedings following a spouse's death.

Prenuptial agreements are not for everyone. Some people view them as unromantic and pessimistic, twisting the wedding vow to cherish one another "until death do us part" into a cold-hearted exit plan.

Others view premarital contracts more pragmatically, mainly when the marriage introduces children from a previous relationship. The more affluent of the two parties may prefer, very reasonably, the security of a known outcome in the event of death or divorce. To that individual (perhaps a wealthy retiree or business owner), the prenup may be an essential ingredient to a successful marriage.

Regardless, prenuptial agreements must always be voluntary.

CHAPTER 2
WHY GET A PRENUPTIAL AGREEMENT?

THERE ARE many reasons couples should consider whether a premarital agreement (prenuptial agreement) might benefit them. Even if their final decision is "No, it is not for us," the conversation is well worth having.

If you are wondering if a premarital agreement would be helpful in your situation, you may be concerned that:

1. Such agreements are unromantic;
2. Your fiancé may feel that you lack trust; or
3. That you lack the desire to enter an equal partnership.

A premarital agreement addresses numerous aspects of married life. The process of negotiating terms and conditions is beneficial in many ways too. One of the reasons it is helpful is that it opens the door for thoughtful, honest communication about a shared future. Open communication is an essential ingredient in a successful marriage.

HAVE A PREMARITAL AGREEMENT CONVERSATION

Having handled hundreds if not thousands of divorces in my career, I have thought on multiple occasions that engaged couples should understand the impact marriage will have on their property, both with and without a premarital agreement.

Unlike business partners, often the divorcing couple entered a legal partnership without the benefit of a partnership agreement (a premarital agreement). This understanding is essential for marriage, estate planning, and divorce.

Myths about community property and separate property are quickly dispelled with knowledge and answers to questions such as:

1. If I deposit my paychecks in a separate account, are they my separate property?
2. Is my pension a separate or community asset?

Couples do not always realize they are forming a 50/50 partnership in Texas when they marry and reside here. In Texas, under the law, the default status for earnings and debts incurred during the marriage is community property. Often, the impact of community property law may seem unfair to the higher-earning spouse. The effect of probate law may also seem unfair to the economically disadvantaged spouse. A well-drafted premarital agreement can help to balance a couple's concerns.

MANAGING FINANCES

Dissatisfaction over marital finances can put tremendous stress on a relationship. We know this, yet couples seldom broach the subject before getting married. One spouse may be a saver, the other a compulsive shopper. Or perhaps both are compulsive shoppers, prone to get into debt quickly. Even when both are savers, one may not save enough in the opinion of the other.

Preparing a premarital agreement forces a discussion about managing marital finances. Each needs to know what he or she is getting into with the other's money habits. Then they can decide how, as a couple, they might adjust their behaviors to be more compatible.

COMBINING RELATIONS

Seldom is avoiding conflict easy when there is tension between a new spouse and the party's children from a previous marriage or relationship.

Whether the children are minors or adults, a premarital agreement may be instructive following a spouse's death. When parties respond emotionally, relationships can sour quickly when the decedent's children oppose the surviving spouse in probate. Terms agreed to in the premarital agreement can clarify what the surviving spouse is entitled to receive, avoiding a costly, contested probate action.

UNDERSTANDING PROPERTY

It is important to understand what actions transform one spouse's separate assets into community property owned by both of the spouses. The spouse who brings substantial wealth to the marriage may be concerned about preserving that wealth, for example, to benefit his or her children from a previous marriage.

MAINTAINING CONTROL

Rather than requiring spouses to follow Texas' Community Property system, the premarital agreement puts them in control of how their assets and liabilities will be shared. This also gives them greater flexibility in how they will provide for one another. For instance, terms of the amount of spousal maintenance or the duration of spousal maintenance can be agreed upon in the event of divorce.

SAVING RESOURCES

The cost of hiring lawyers to prepare the premarital agreement is typically less, often substantially less, expensive than incurring the expense of litigating a divorce or contested probate action. Should the relationship fall apart, the premarital agreement can save time and costs by providing for a clear, orderly disposition of accumulated wealth and debts.

In the absence of a premarital agreement, Texas's divorce statutes and case law will only provide general guidelines. This makes specific results at trial unpredictable. Uncertainty of outcome is an essential factor in leading people to risk litigation over the settlement. However, litigation always comes at a high cost.

Although rare, parties can execute a premarital agreement and have a marriage annulled. There are many grounds for annulment of marriage under Texas Family Code Section 6, including:

1. Certain underage marriages;
2. At least one of the spouses was under the influence of drugs or alcohol at the time of the marriage and could not consent to the marriage;
3. Undisclosed impotency discovered after the marriage;
4. Fraud, duress, or force;
5. Mental incapacity;
6. Concealed divorce.

WHAT HAPPENS TO A PREMARITAL AGREEMENT WHEN A MARRIAGE IS ANNULLED?

Texas Family Code Section 4.007 says, "If a marriage is determined to be void, an agreement that would otherwise have been a premarital agreement is enforceable only to the extent necessary to avoid an inequitable result."

Do the points listed above mirror your concerns or pique an

interest in the potential benefits of negotiating a marriage future? Keep reading. The next step is to determine how you and your future spouse might benefit from a premarital agreement.

WHO NEEDS A PREMARITAL AGREEMENT?

A prenuptial agreement is an action plan of the parties' own making. The deal includes terms and conditions effective upon the passing of specified events. For instance, an agreed term may provide:

1. The economically dependent spouse a predetermined amount of spousal maintenance if they legally separate or divorce;
2. An agreed condition, maybe the planned purchase of a vacation home, can only follow a debt-free marital residence;
3. An express statement of each spouse's portion of the mortgage payment.

What is the takeaway? It is essential to have flexibility and control over what happens with the marriage down the road. Ten years or so in the future (with married life no longer hypothetical), the spouses could choose to modify their premarital agreement, revoke it in its entirety, create a superseding premarital agreement, or do nothing at all.

CONSIDERATIONS WORTHY OF NEGOTIATION

To retain flexibility and control tomorrow, give marriage careful consideration today. Marriage is a huge commitment. Planning an idyllic wedding is exciting, a lifetime experience that should be joyful and memorable. But negotiating terms and conditions for a premarital agreement means imagining what this marriage could be and should be. That is not a simple task. Start the conversation by raising the following questions.

ASSETS AND DEBTS

Is a premarital agreement to protect significant assets? Is there a substantial imbalance of wealth or income? Are circumstances such that one will bring considerable debt to the marriage? What percentage of revenue will each spouse apply to fund an IRA, 401k, or another retirement plan?

Involving a certified financial advisor or Certified Public Accountant (CPA), with their lawyer's assistance, may be necessary for fruitful negotiations between parties.

CHILDREN

Is this a second marriage for either party? Does either party have children from a previous marriage or relationship? What is the plan for raising a child? Creating a plan for the child's treatment during the marriage, in the event of divorce, or upon a parent's death will take careful consideration. Be sure to build #exibility and control into the premarital agreement.

PROFESSIONAL PRACTICES OR BUSINESS INTERESTS

Is either party a business owner? In the absence of a prenuptial agreement, a business with a community interest is divided upon divorce or upon the death of the spouse who Was the primary operator. This could mean the termination of the organization and the end of a steady income stream. Consider, too, the consequences of dividing a professional practice as a marital asset.

RETIREMENT AGES

What about age? Is one party significantly older than the other? On the wedding day, the younger spouse may have many earning-years ahead while the older spouse is already drawing a pension or approaching retirement on a fixed income.

Lovers may not care much about age differences, but age disparity may be cause for financial concern. If divorce results in equal, or nearly equal, division of community assets and debts, then the older spouse's financial resources may never be sufficiently recovered to provide for his or her retirement.

Each spouse owns one half of the community estate (assets and debts). Could that division be altered? Yes, by a premarital agreement negotiated before marriage or by agreement during a divorce.

A valid premarital agreement may include a property division plan that deviates from the presumed division of 50/50 under Texas law and plans for the elder spouse's late-in-life needs.

COLLEGE AND PROFESSIONAL DEGREES

Might one spouse willingly support the other, so their marriage benefits from future income generated through the other spouse's college or professional degrees? One spouse may work two or three jobs to cover household and tuition expenses. Doing so allows the other spouse to concentrate on coursework and focus on obtaining the degree that will, they believe, ultimately benefit the marital community. Sometimes spouses postpone having children as well.

What is a fair division of property if this couple gets divorced or separates? Or upon death, how should the decedent's estate be shared? What if survivors include the decedent's children from a previous marriage? Again, a prenup is about control with flexibility.

INHERITANCES AND GIFTS

What happens if a spouse anticipates receiving a substantial inheritance during the marriage? A provision in the premarital agreement could determine how inheritance is handled upon a spouse's death. The premarital agreement could provide that any estate remains the beneficiary's separate property despite their actions during the marriage. In the absence of a premarital agreement, the future activities of the spouse could risk the inheritance being construed as transmutation, or a gift to the community under Texas law.

With an experienced Family Law attorney's help during negotiations, drafting, and execution, a premarital agreement can resolve these and other complex issues. When the time arrives to enforce the agreement, the attorney knows that the Court must determine whether all substantive terms are fair and whether procedural fairness existed in negotiating and executing the contract before the wedding.

CHAPTER 3
OPINIONS AND CONCERNS REGARDING PREMARITAL AGREEMENTS

THERE ARE many opinions and concerns when it comes to premarital agreements. These opinions are sometimes based on facts but are more often based on emotions. When it comes to the subject of getting married these emotions are understandable. This chapter will focus on discussing some of these emotional concerns.

YOU ONLY CARE ABOUT MONEY

One concern that I often hear is that if you are asking for a premarital agreement, it means you only care about money. Another question I hear a lot is "why are you planning for a divorce?" Something to consider is that marriage is very much a partnership in every sense of the word, including finances.

The subject of money should not be looked at as a negative aspect of marriage. The topic is just a part of life. Just like in a business partnership, if both partners are not on board on how to handle

finances this can create friction when partners are moving in different directions. One of the goals of a premarital agreement is to help couples enter the marriage with a complete understanding of the finances and how they will be handled in the marriage.

YOU DO NOT TRUST ME

Another excuse I have heard is that asking for a premarital agreement is an indication that the person asking for one has trust issues. However, I think the discussion process involved in the creation of a premarital agreement helps create trust. Discussing a premarital agreement is an opportunity to proactively discuss how finances and property will be handled as it comes into the marriage or is acquired. This allows trust to be built by listening to the ideas of a couple to ensure everyone is on the same page.

PREMARITAL AGREEMENTS JUST PREPARE FOR A DIVORCE

A sentiment I frequently hear is that people feel that having a premarital agreement is planning for a divorce. However, by creating a premarital agreement the couple has outlined a road map for their future together. A premarital agreement encourages a couple to discuss their expectations for the marriage and how it will work. This plan involves how to handle financial and other marital issues.

Premarital agreements are not new; they have existed for centuries. They have been used for outlining the roles and responsibilities of the marriage. There are several different examples of these agreements throughout history.

Marriage counselors have pointed out that failure to communicate and money issues are two of the main reasons that marriages fail. The process of discussing and potentially developing a premarital agreement allows couples the opportunity to talk about and evaluate their thoughts and ideas and to it come to an understanding of each other's viewpoints about finances and the marital relationship.

CHAPTER 4

TERMS AND CONDITIONS IN PREMARITAL AGREEMENTS

A PREMARITAL AGREEMENT (prenuptial agreement) can be beneficial in terms of planning for a compatible and stable married life. But some things are strictly o"-limits. Couples cannot agree to an act that violates public policy. Nor can they contract to do something criminal or illegal. For example, an "agreement" to commit tax evasion by hiding earnings from the IRS could never be enforced in Court by one spouse against the other.

Texas Statutes list the scope of what is permissible with a premarital agreement and what is expressly prohibited. The language of Texas Family Code Section 4.003 (a) is broad and allows the parties to negotiate reasonable terms with substantial flexibility:

1. the rights and obligations of each of the parties in any of the property of either or both of them whenever and wherever acquired or located;
2. the right to buy, sell, use, transfer, exchange, abandon, lease, consume, expend, assign, create a security interest in, mortgage, encumber, dispose of, or otherwise manage and control property;

3. the disposition of property on separation, marital dissolution, death, or the occurrence or nonoccurrence of any other event;
4. the modification or elimination of spousal support;
5. the making of a will, trust, or other arrangements to carry out the provisions of the agreement;
6. the ownership rights in and disposition of the death benefit from a life insurance policy;
7. the choice of law governing the construction of the agreement; and
8. any other matter, including their personal rights and obligations, not in violation of public policy or a statute imposing a criminal penalty.

(b) The right of child support may not be adversely affected by a premarital agreement.

What does a prenup look like on paper? Here are twelve everyday items that couples request in their Texas premarital agreements:

PROPERTY

Premarital agreement terms and conditions regarding the property, both separate and community. Treatment of assets and debts during a marriage, including income, earnings, any "interest, present or future, legal or equitable, vested or contingent," and real property, makes up a large portion of Texas Premarital Agreements.

PERSONAL PROPERTY

Not only are couples free to determine how property will be purchased, sold, used, transferred, mortgaged, and managed during the marriage, but they may also decide how property will be divided in the event of separation or divorce. Before they marry, couples are free to negotiate the division of community property, valuation of assets, and allocation of debts.

Many important decisions need to be made before the wedding. Who will keep the house? How will the mortgage be paid? Who gets which investment fund? Who shall have a controlling interest in the family business? Both spouses work from the same game plan on marriage, separation, divorce, and untimely death of a spouse. Similar to a separation agreement settling property division in divorce, they may characterize future assets and debts as either separate or community property.

REAL ESTATE

You purchased your house before you met your fiancé. After the wedding, you probably will both reside in the home. In the event of a divorce, is this property a marital or separate property asset? To avoid the gray area that family homes can fall into, putting in place a premarital agreement is an easy way to legally outline home ownership and what will happen to the home in the event of a divorce. For this reason, decisions concerning a home that one spouse owned before marriage are one of the most common items listed in most premarital agreements.

RETIREMENT ACCOUNTS

Be aware that most retirement and pension accounts in Texas are subject to the state's community property rule. With this in mind, it's common to see language in premarital agreements exempting retirement accounts from consideration as community property or fixing a certain percentage/split if the couple does divorce.

Under Texas Family Code Section 7.001 GENERAL RULE OF PROPERTY DIVISION:

"In a decree of divorce or annulment, the court shall order a division of the estate of the parties in a manner that the court deems just and right, having due regard for the rights of each party and any children of the marriage."

Case law has mostly found that "just and right" means that the starting point for dividing community property is 50/50. However, with a premarital agreement, either individual may waive their future marital interest in the other's IRA, pension, or 401k funded with matrimonial earnings. If the premarital agreement waives the right to a community share of the other spouse's retirement asset, then upon death or divorce, the retirement asset is, by contract, not marital property.

PROVIDING FOR SPOUSAL MAINTENANCE

In the event of a divorce, how much will you pay or receive in alimony? What if one of you becomes ill and can no longer work throughout your marriage? What if your spouse cheats? What about spousal income loss when one spouse stays home to raise the children? Instead of monthly payments, would a lump sum or equivalent (assigning over homeownership, for example) be an acceptable alternative? Many couples choose to make decisions about alimony now rather than fight about it later.

Most challenges to premarital agreements involve spousal support, usually because the couple accumulated more during the marriage, and the premarital agreement does not account for those assets.

Texas law allows for agreements to modify or eliminate spousal maintenance (alimony) of a spouse. These are standard clauses in a premarital agreement. An individual may waive the right to financial support from their spouse in the event of separation or divorce in the future.

SEPARATION OF BUSINESS INTERESTS

You own a business. In the event of a divorce, can your spouse claim a part or percent, even if he or she did not participate in it? To keep businesses and business shares out of the divorce, a premarital agreement can clearly define these types of investments and income as separate or can outline the specific percentage a spouse would be entitled to claim.

ASSETS EARMARKED FOR CHILDREN

If you have children from a previous relationship and know you would like certain assets you currently own to be inherited by these children (i.e., money, stocks, furniture, or other real property), a premarital agreement can include language listing which specific property is to be kept separate for their interest.

BANK ACCOUNTS & CREDIT CARDS

Have a hefty savings account, or vice versa, have a wonderful spouse-to-be who made the mistake of over-spending on his or her credit cards a few years back? A prenuptial agreement can specify these types of separate items — individual bank accounts and personal debt — remain separate in the event of a divorce, rather than being open to division.

PERSONAL PROPERTY

Antiques? Your collection of beer mugs? The furniture you bought solo before marriage? To avoid confusion in the event of a divorce, outlining ownership of personal property in the premarital agreement can save much haggling and heartache down the road.

PETS

Your pet has been by your side for years, but after years of marriage, could your spouse claim ownership? Since pets for some couples are as dear as children, it's no surprise here that outlining pet ownership in a premarital agreement is becoming more and more common.

ATTORNEY FEES AND COSTS

The parties to a premarital agreement can also negotiate who pays the cost of preparing the premarital agreement. This is incredibly helpful when a wealthy individual wants a premarital agreement to get married. Still, the other party needs financial assistance to hire his or her own attorney. As discussed later, having one's own attorney to negotiate and draft the premarital agreement is paramount. If the financially dominant party wholly controls the negotiation and the other party cannot afford to obtain review by independent counsel, enforcement may become problematic.

What is the point of an invalid or unenforceable premarital agreement? It is essential to get things right from the beginning.

The agreement may also provide for:

1. The payment of legal fees;
2. Court costs;
3. Forensic calculations;
4. Child custody evaluations; and
5. Related expenses in a divorce.

Additionally, the couple can agree on how probate costs and expenses related to the administration of the decedent's estate will be paid. Will the costs be paid from community resources, for instance, or from the deceased spouse's separate bank or investment account?

TAXATION MATTERS

A premarital agreement may include provisions addressing tax matters. The parties could designate responsibility for preparing a joint tax return, especially if one party is more sophisticated or has specialized expertise or training in that area. They may agree upon the portion each will contribute to the payment of taxes if, for example, one's income is substantially higher than the other's. Couples might agree that each will be responsible for the taxes owed on separate property income and pay the tax owed from a different bank account. At the same time, they agree to keep income earned on separate property segregated for tax purposes.

Deciding how tax matters will be handled in marriage is why you consult a CPA or tax attorney. Before accepting any arrangement, understand current law and how the proposed premarital agreement alters the outcome.

For example, previously, if a higher-earning spouse was to pay alimony, it represented a tax break for the payor. The recipient included the alimony as income and was assessed the tax, but at a lower rate, perhaps much lower. During negotiations, the deduction incentivized paying more to support a dependent spouse who enjoyed a lower tax rate.

However, things changed on January 1, 2019. There is no longer an alimony deduction. It is important to be mindful that the laws on these and other family law issues could change at any time.

ON THE CHILD'S UPBRINGING

Some couples include terms and conditions in a premarital agreement attempting to control custody upon a parent's death or divorce. Child custody is a general term meant to include legal decision-making authority and parent access to the child. Custody issues are not something that can be constrained by using a premarital agreement.

Why is that? A premarital agreement cannot limit a party's constitutionally protected parental rights. The right to parent one's child is within the Fifth and Fourteen Amendments' due process clauses in the United States Constitution. The premarital agreement is also prohibited from providing a parenting plan that is not in the child's best interest.

NO-CHILD PROVISIONS

Currently, there are no cases represented in Texas regarding these provisions. However, premarital agreements containing no-child requirements, where the parties agree not to have children together, are becoming increasingly prevalent. More women are choosing long-term careers and marrying later in life.

TEXAS CUSTODY LAW PREVALENCE

Texas custody law takes precedence over the premarital agreement with child custody terms. Couples cannot use the premarital agreement to dictate parenting time or who shall have the legal decision-making authority over a child if they separate or divorce. That is for the Court to determine based upon statutory factors weighted according to the child's best interest.

Furthermore, the premarital agreement cannot divest the Court of custody jurisdiction over a minor child. Parents should negotiate a parenting plan in good faith, with their attorneys' assistance, and submit their parenting plan to the Court.

A couple might want to provide personal guidance for married life by reciting custody intentions, for example, stating their mutual desire for joint custody and equal parenting time if they divorce. They might agree to one parent being the primary caregiver who works from home until they reach a certain age. What if the parent chooses a different career path? That is his or her right. Could the other spouse sue to enforce a premarital agreement that requires the other parent to work from home or not at all? No.

Understand that some wishes affect personal rights and obligations and, as such, are not enforceable and will not bind the judge in divorce proceedings. In any case, such a provision should be made severable from the premarital agreement without affecting the overall validity and enforceability of the agreement's remaining terms and conditions.

EDUCATION

Provisions directing the child's upbringing and education may be included in a premarital agreement, although court enforcement might not always be possible. Compare a requirement over education with a provision over religious upbringing.

A contract stating that a child attends a private school and receives private lessons in music and arts may be enforceable in divorce proceedings.

RELIGION

However, an agreement on the child's religious upbringing may not be enforceable. Courts generally do not interfere with a parent's decision to expose the child to a spiritual practice or belief that, standing alone, violates the premarital agreement's religious upbringing provision.

The Court in *Zummo v. Zummo* 574 A.2d 1130, 1144 (Pa. Super. 1990) considered the enforcement of a religious clause in a premarital agreement. Within this case, an observant Jewish mother and a lapsed Catholic father were divorcing. The father disputed a clause stating he was barred from taking his children to religious services other than Jewish, despite the fact that prior to marriage, the couple had agreed to raise the children in the Jewish faith. The Court noted that:

1. Such contracts are generally too vague to demonstrate a meeting of minds or to provide an adequate basis for objective enforcement;
2. Enforcement of such an agreement would promote a particular religion, serve little or no secular purpose, and would excessively entangle the courts in religious matters; and
3. Enforcement would be contrary to a public policy embodied in the First Amendment Establishment and Free Exercises Clauses...that parents be free to doubt, question, and change their beliefs, and that they be free to instruct their children in accordance with those beliefs.

An exception to this general rule would be if there were substantial risks of actual harm to the child from the religious practice or belief.

ADDITIONAL CHILD SUPPORT

Can a couple provide for child support obligations and amounts in their premarital agreement? Under Texas law, a premarital agreement cannot adversely impact child support. For instance, the contract cannot determine which parent will be wholly responsible for paying child support. Parties can agree on extra help for private lessons, extracurricular activities, travel, and so on.

With every custody proceeding, the Court will order child support based upon calculations using the Texas Child Support Guidelines. No child should be made to suffer for lack of support simply because their parents entered into a premarital agreement with terms contrary to guidelines.

Future parents can agree to child support over that required by Guidelines but cannot reduce or eliminate child support in violation of Guidelines. For example, they could decide the wealthier parent should provide additional monthly support, paying child-related expenses for extracurricular activities, and funding a college trust. But couples cannot agree to eliminate or diminish a parent's legal obligation to support their child.

Generally, a premarital agreement cannot negatively impact third parties' rights to the agreement, such as the creditor of one or both spouses. A child may enforce a provision in the understanding that creates a beneficial right in the child as a third party beneficiary. Say the premarital agreement included a provision to fund a college trust, as an example. Still, the parents either failed to pay into the trust or removed funds from the educational trust for some reason.

CHAPTER 5
WHAT IS REQUIRED FOR VALIDITY OF A PREMARITAL AGREEMENT?

THE VALIDITY of a premarital agreement must be proven in Court if it's relevant to the outcome of a contested divorce or probate proceeding. A contest can occur when one party, for example, desires spousal maintenance in divorce and challenges the premarital provision eliminating the other spouse's obligation to pay. The best way to make sure a court will uphold the terms of a premarital agreement is to do your homework and make sure that every procedural and substantive step is in place and followed appropriately.

PREMARITAL AGREEMENT FORMALITIES

FIRST, a premarital agreement must be in writing and signed by both parties. Additionally, a prenup only becomes valid after the marriage takes place, so it doesn't apply to called-o" engagements. According to the Texas Family Code, a premarital agreement is not enforceable if:

1. One or both spouses did not sign the agreement voluntarily; or

2. The agreement was unconscionable when it was signed, meaning a spouse was not provided a fair and reasonable disclosure of the property or financial obligations of the other party, did not voluntarily waive, in writing, the right to disclosure of the property or financial obligations of the other party, and didn't have adequate knowledge of the property or financial obligations of the other party.

As discussed previously, premarital agreements are a unique type of contract. One particular characteristic is that consideration per se (something of value given in exchange for a promise) is not required, as noted above, to bind the parties to the agreement. A binding contract allows the Court to enforce it against the violating party. Still, many argue the promise to marry is adequate consideration when exchanged for a promise to sign a premarital agreement. With consideration satisfied, the remaining requirements for validity are the legal capacity to contract and voluntariness.

LEGAL CAPACITY TO CONTRACT

Does the person have a requisite legal capacity to enter a premarital agreement? If the premarital agreement is challenged in the parties' divorce, for instance, the Court will look back to the circumstances surrounding the contract's execution.

A party to an agreement must have the ability to understand:

1. Nature;
2. Extent;
3. Character; and
4. Effect of the agreement.

He or she must be able to understand what signing the agreement reasonably will do in terms of limiting or waiving marital rights. The ability to understand the contract and the actual understanding of the contract are two distinct concepts.

CONTRACTING MUST HAVE BEEN VOLUNTARY

A contract must be voluntary. Premarital agreements are, by their very nature, prone to being executed under emotional circumstances. For some, marriage may not happen at all if the premarital agreement goes unsigned. Therefore, the courts look more closely at the requirement that it is a voluntarily entered contract and not something else. Neither party can waive the provision of voluntariness.

While Sections 4.006 and 4.105 of the Texas Family Code do not define "voluntarily," courts have generally construed it to mean an action that is taken intentionally or by the free exercise of one's will. *Martin v. Martin*, 287 S.W.3d 260 (Tex. App.–Dallas 2009, pet. denied)

What does involuntariness look like? Ultimately, it means an individual was coerced into signing the agreement. Coercion may be through:

1. Fraud;
2. Duress;
3. Undue influence; or
4. Overreaching.

FACTORS CONSIDERED WHEN DETERMINING IF INVOLUNTARINESS EXISTED

One Court in *Moore v. Moore*, 383 S.W.3d 190 (Tex. App.–Dallas 2012, no pet. h.) considered when determining whether any evidence of involuntariness existed:

1. whether a party has had the advice of counsel;
2. misrepresentations made in procuring the agreement;

3. the amount of information provided; and
4. whether information has been withheld.

UNDUE INFLUENCE

Undue influence means the individual is coerced into signing the contract by another's unlawful threat. Because of that threat, the weaker party had no alternative but to sign the agreement.

When undue influence destroys voluntariness, the individual was deprived of any meaningful choice. The will of another usually the other party to the premarital agreement, but not always) effectively replaced his or her freedom of choice to decide whether to execute the agreement or not.

For instance, the parties' relationship may involve a weaker individual who is emotionally and financially controlled by a dominant partner, or an overbearing parent who desires the premarital agreement. Undue influence is always something to look for among those in a close relationship such as:

1. Family,
2. Friends,
3. Coworkers, and
4. Two people planning to spend married life together.

FAIRNESS IS NEEDED

Texas Family Code Section 4.006 requires that for premarital agreements to be valid, they must be fair both procedurally and substantively. To satisfy procedural fairness, voluntariness is needed. With substantive fairness, if the contract was unconscionable when signed, then it should be held invalid.

What does unconscionability mean in this context? An unconscionable agreement shocks the conscience or is expressly unconscionable, according to the Statute. The judge determines unconscionable as a question of law under section 4.006(c) of the Texas Family Code.

A valid premarital agreement is supported by fair and reasonable disclosure of both individuals' property or financial obligations. Substantive unfairness may result if there was inadequate or nonexistent financial disclosure of assets and debts.

The most common situation of substantive unfairness involves a party who did not know, and could not have known, about the other's finances. Without a property disclosure, the agreement may be unconscionable, lacking substantive fairness from the beginning under Section 4.006(2)(A) of the Texas Family Code. Unlike voluntariness, however, a party can waive the right to fair disclosure and proper financial disclosure under Section 4.006(2)(B).

STEPS TO PREVENT ARGUMENTS AGAINST ENFORCEMENT OF A PREMARITAL AGREEMENT

For these reasons, both parties must fully disclose all earnings, property, and financial obligations during a premarital agreement negotiation. If one spouse proves that the other hid an asset, a source of income, or a financial obligation, this will create an argument against the agreement's enforcement. If the agreement were based on information that was inaccurate in some way, this would prove an argument against enforcement.

Sometimes the lack of adequate time to review and consider information could support an argument that a fiancé could not reasonably have had sufficient knowledge of the property or financial obligations. This can be avoided by allowing time to review all disclosures and the agreement.

If one party retains an attorney to draft the agreement, the other party must have adequate time and opportunity to hire an attorney to review the deal and provide legal advice.

CHAPTER 6
PROVING VOLUNTARINESS IN THE COURTROOM

ARE you familiar with the adage, "It is not a problem until it is a problem?" With most spouses, the premarital agreement does not undergo judicial scrutiny for years, perhaps decades, after its execution. The problem spouses encounter is when they discover potential vulnerabilities with the contract when enforcement is sought by one or both parties. As with any agreement, the ideal time to make corrections and adjustments is after review by independent counsel and before signing it. However, that is not how things always play out.

Problems with the premarital agreement surface quickly when one party asks the Court to enforce it while the other party objects on one or more grounds. A challenge initiates multi-factor analysis by the Court, something a bit more in-depth than establishing "who drafted it?"

STATUTE OF LIMITATIONS

Enforcement of the premarital agreement in probate or family court often occurs many years after the instrument was signed. By contrast, with a breach of contract or personal injury lawsuit, the years that passed without the plaintiff taking any legal action would result in dismissal because the complaint was "led too late, outside of that statute of limitation period.

With the enforcement of a premarital agreement, though, marriage tolls the clock for allowing a spouse to sue and enforce the premarital agreement decades after the agreement was entered into. A special limitation period exists for premarital agreements under the Texas Family Code Section 4.008:

LIMITATION OF ACTIONS. A statute of limitations applicable to an action asserting a claim for relief under a premarital agreement is tolled during the marriage of the parties to the agreement. However, equitable defenses limiting the time for enforcement, including laches and estoppel, are available to either party.

Consequently, arguments that premarital agreement enforcement should be time-barred are only available in equity. Those equitable defenses include:

1. Laches because of the spouse's unreasonable delay in seeking premarital agreement enforcement;
2. Estoppel, given the spouse's previous conduct; and
3. The spouse's unclean hands for having acted in bad faith, among others.

LACHES

For laches to apply, the proponent must establish that a party unreasonably delayed asserting their rights and that this delay caused the proponent to change their legal position in good faith, to their detriment, because of the delay.

An example of a case where laches were applied was in *Fazakerly*, 996 S.W.2.D. 265. A daughter, with knowledge of a premarital agreement between her deceased father and her stepmother, signed a settlement agreement with her stepmother and then waited five years to contest the premarital agreement. The stepmother developed

Alzheimer's during the intervening period and was no longer competent to testify about the premarital agreement.

ESTOPPEL

This is a defense that can be raised, for example, if the party had made representations that caused the delay in "ling suit after the limitations period had run.

WHO CARRIES THE BURDEN OF PROOF IN COURT?

When a premarital agreement's validity is challenged in a divorce or probate action, the responsibility for carrying the burden of proof is an essential aspect of a case.

At the trial or hearing, the Court opens with the legal presumption the spouses' premarital agreement is valid. From there, the spouse challenging the validity of the premarital agreement carries the initial burden of proof and must make a case of the agreement's invalidity. The burden of proof then shifts to the proponent of the premarital agreement, who must offer evidence of the premarital agreement's validity. The judge will analyze the agreement regarding voluntariness.

TEXAS LAW FOR AGREEMENTS MADE ON OR BEFORE SEPTEMBER 1, 1993

In 1993, the legislature amended the Family Code by eliminating common-law defenses to the enforcement of premarital agreements executed on or after September 1, 1993. Thus, for premarital agreements executed on or after September 1, 1993, involuntary execution and unconscionability are the only grounds for contesting the enforcement of a premarital agreement.

Tex. Fam. Code §4.006(c). While Family Code §4.006(c) indicates that involuntary execution and unconscionability are the exclusive defenses to enforcement of a premarital agreement, a specific term of an agreement (as opposed to the agreement as a whole) can still be challenged if it is a prohibited contractual term.

VOLUNTARINESS FACTORS

With a divorce or probate pending, the premarital agreement's validity may be challenged by either spouse, by a deceased spouse's executor, or by a third-party beneficiary of the contract. A premarital agreement could be set aside for a number of reasons.

Factors that the Court should consider when determining whether the agreement was voluntarily entered into include:

1. Advice of Counsel,
2. Misrepresentation,
3. Amount of information, and
4. Withheld information.

INDEPENDENT LEGAL ADVICE

Several Texas courts have held that lack of separate representation does not make an agreement unenforceable, for example, *Marsh v. Marsh*, 949 S.W.2d 734 (Tex. App.–Houston 1997, no writ).

Although having an attorney is not required for a premarital agreement to be valid, obtaining independent legal counsel is an indicator of voluntariness. It is also probably the single most crucial factor supporting voluntariness when the contract is challenged in Court by a spouse.

The best practice would be for both fiancés to have attorneys and to participate in drawing up the premarital agreement.

What if the attorney's recommendation was "do not sign the premarital agreement as written?" The lawyer's guidance was still independent legal advice despite the client's rejection.

What if the drafting party recommended the other fiancé obtain legal advice before deciding whether or not to sign the agreement? Still, the other party rejected the recommendation and signed without a lawyer reviewing the agreement? Knowing and having the opportunity to obtain independent legal advice will be evidence of voluntariness.

MISREPRESENTATION

The Court may consider whether any misrepresentations were made in obtaining the agreement. Was there any fraud to induce the party to sign the premarital agreement? Did a party materially misrepresent his or her property and debts? Misrepresentation occurs when a party misleads or hides assets or liabilities from the other party.

AMOUNT OF INFORMATION

A court may also consider how much information was provided prior to the signing of the agreement. Parties to a premarital agreement may include a recital or statement about how they know everything they need to know and how they made financial disclosure before executing the contract.

Full financial disclosure of assets and debts is essential, but the right to fair and reasonable disclosure of property and financial obligations may be waived. Not surprisingly, the waiver must be voluntary, express, and in writing.

There are various ways to make sufficient financial disclosures:

1. Itemized statements,
2. Statements of net worth,
3. Income summary,
4. Provision of financial records,
5. Verbal exchange of financial information,
6. Business profit and loss statement, and
7. Informal disclosure providing "constructive knowledge."

Constructive knowledge is based upon pre-existing informally obtained financial information. Knowledge is gathered by observation and communications occurring before and during the couple's courtship. Relying on the outward appearance of someone's lifestyle without concrete evidence of net worth and income should be avoided.

WITHHELD INFORMATION

The Court can consider whether any information was withheld from the parties signing the agreement. A person may enjoy a high standard of living but be massively in debt, hence the need for full disclosure of property and finances.

Worse, a carefully planned façade of wealth could rise to the level of intentional fraud. If a spouse was purposely inducing a fiancé into marriage by rubbing elbows with the right people and appearing on exclusive occasions, this could be considered fraud.

Conversely, someone who appears to be of modest means may, in fact, be quite wealthy. Sam Walton, the founder of Walmart, even after becoming a billionaire, drove a pickup truck and wore clothes from his own discount store. Looks can be deceiving.

EVIDENCE OF FRAUD DURESS, UNDUE INFLUENCE

Whether Texas courts can consider evidence of fraud, duress, and undue influence in determining an involuntary execution of a premarital agreement is uncertain. This is due to the Texas Family Code, which makes involuntary execution and unconscionability the exclusive defenses to a premarital agreement as of September 1, 1993. Courts agree that these defenses can be considered for agreements made on or before September 1, 1993. They are less certain for agreements made after.

Whether there was overreaching, duress, or undue influence

depends upon the circumstances and is not always obvious. Consider the voluntariness of the following circumstances:

THREATS

Were there threats? Duress includes a threat of violence, which would be persuasive evidence of involuntariness. By contrast, threatening not to marry unless a premarital agreement is signed is not compelling evidence.

COMPETENCY

Competency is a question of whether a person could understand the agreement. Did the spouse have the legal capacity to contract at the time he or she signed the agreement? Was he or she mentally incompetent at the time? Did the spouse sign the premarital agreement under the influence of drugs or alcohol?

TIMING

When the premarital agreement was presented for execution is yet another essential factor when considering voluntariness. Generally, premarital agreements should be finalized as far in advance of the wedding date as possible.

An agreement executed too close to the wedding date has a higher probability of being challenged on the grounds of duress or undue influence. However, several Texas cases have upheld premarital agreements that were executed close in time to the wedding, for example, Williams v. Williams, 720 S.W.2d 246 (Tex. App.–Houston [14th Dist.] 1986, no writ).

A better plan would be to allow sufficient time for a reasonable reflection. What is considered a reasonable time may depend on the circumstances involved.

KNOWLEDGE OF MARITAL RIGHTS

The voluntariness factor also considers the importance of obtaining independent legal advice and knowing the fiancé's financial situation. This involves the couple knowing how Texas Law handles Marital Rights and Obligations without a premarital agreement.

Generally, the most significant impact is usually on community property rights and alimony. A waiver of these rights must be voluntary for a premarital agreement to be enforced against the waiving spouse.

There are limits on what a fiancé can waive. Before signing any agreement, discuss those rights and obligations with a lawyer.

PREGNANCY

It is not persuasive for the woman to be so worried about being pregnant that she signed the premarital agreement.

LANGUAGE FLUENCY

With a potential language barrier, as with an immigrant who is not fluent in English, the requisite communication level in English sufficient to support validity is low.

EMOTIONAL RESISTANT

It is not enough for a spouse to testify in Court that "I did not want to sign the agreement." A party with emotional opposition to signing the premarital agreement, but who does so anyway, is not considered evidence of involuntariness.

VIDEO RECORDING

Video recording the signing ceremony could ensure the enforceability of a premarital or postmarital agreement. A video recording may provide evidence of a lack of duress and involuntariness should a disagreement later arise.

TESTIMONY BEFORE A COURT REPORTER

Either in conjunction with a video recorded signing ceremony or separately, having a court reporter swear in the parties to the premarital agreement and asking them questions on the record about duress, voluntariness, and understanding of the contract may provide evidence should a party attempt to contest the agreement in the future.

UNEQUAL BARGAINING POWER

This is not persuasive because premarital agreements almost always involve an imbalance of bargaining power. Negotiating a fair deal is a key reason why both individuals should obtain legal advice.

ORAL PROMISES

Verbal agreements that were never written into the premarital agreement are not persuasive evidence of involuntariness. However, on the issue of whether a party's waiver was involuntary, it may be useful to show in advance the written document presentation for the party's signing.

DELIBERATE IGNORANCE

What if a party was adequately presented with the agreement but opted not to read it? Choosing not to read the premarital agreement before signing it is a personal choice. However, failure to read the document and choosing to sign it is not persuasive evidence of an involuntary agreement.

LOVE

Does love change everything? For example, the party who wanted a premarital agreement made extraordinarily generous provisions for their fiancé. But in their divorce, that same spouse argued the premarital agreement should be set aside for undue influence because he was blinded by love. As one might expect, being blinded by love is not persuasive evidence of involuntariness.

UNCONSCIONABLE AT TIME OF EXECUTION

Whether an agreement was unconscionable when it was signed is a question of law. Neither the Family Code nor Texas courts have defined the term "unconscionable" in the context of a premarital agreement (Marsh, 949 S.W.2d at 739; see Tex. Fam. Code §4.001 et seq).

To help define the term, courts have looked to the definition of unconscionability in the commercial context. In the commercial context, an agreement is unconscionable if, given the parties' general backgrounds and their particular needs, the contract is so one-sided that no reasonable person would consider it an arm's-length transaction. The principle underlying the concept of unconscionability is the prevention of oppression and unfair surprise. Courts conduct both a procedural and a substantive review of the contract to determine whether the agreement was unconscionable when it was signed.

PROCEDURAL UNCONSCIONABILITY

Procedural unconscionability focuses on the actual making or inducement of the contract. This form of unconscionability addresses how the parties arrived at the terms of the contract by reviewing the facts surrounding the bargaining process. Under this form of review, courts look at:

1. the presence of deceptive, overreaching, and sharp business practices;
2. the absence of a viable alternative; and
3. the relative understanding, knowledge, education, and financial ability of the parties involved.

SUBSTANTIVE UNCONSCIONABILITY

Substantive unconscionability focuses on the terms and conditions of the agreement. Under the Family Code, the agreement's terms and conditions must be unconscionable when the agreement was signed for the agreement to be unenforceable.

Texas courts had followed the statutory directive, focusing on the circumstances when the agreement was signed, not on any resulting disproportionate effect. For instance, in Marriage of Smith, 115 S.W.3d at 135, although the division of marital property under contract disproportionately favored one spouse, the Court reviewed the circumstances when an agreement was signed, not whether a contract was unconscionable years later.

As a result, an agreement that is simply "unfair" because it disproportionately favors one party over another is not substantively unconscionable.

TEXAS COURTS AND UNCONSCIONABILITY

Texas courts have addressed the issue of unconscionability on a case-by-case basis, looking to the entire atmosphere in which the agreement was made. The simplicity of the statutory language notwithstanding, the determination of "unconscionability" may be quite complex and usually involves a detailed inquiry into the facts and circumstances surrounding a disputed marital agreement.

In determining whether a contract is unconscionable or not, the courts must look to the entire atmosphere in which the agreement was made, the alternatives, if any, which were available to the parties at the time of the making of the contract; the non-bargaining ability of one party; whether the contract is illegal or against public policy; and whether the contract is oppressive or unreasonable.

At the same time, a party who knowingly enters a lawful but improvident contract is not entitled to protection by the courts. In the absence of any mistake, fraud, or oppression, the courts are not interested in the wisdom or policy of contracts and agreements voluntarily entered into between competent and reasonable parties.

CHAPTER 7
AMENDMENTS, REVOCATIONS & POSTMARITAL AGREEMENTS

PREVIOUSLY, we focused on the flexibility and control a well-drafted and thoughtfully negotiated premarital agreement can provide. Still, the spouses may wish to make changes to their agreement after they have been married. They may decide to revoke their agreement.

Can a premarital agreement be changed or terminated after marriage? Yes, so long as all the formalities are followed. Spouses may revoke their agreement. Doing so restores their marital rights under the law and puts them back in the position they would have been in had there been no premarital agreement at all.

Just as the premarital agreement must be in writing, any modifications or revocations of the premarital agreement must be made in writing and must be signed by both spouses. No matter how many times the conversation surfaced over the years, verbalizing a mutual desire to cancel the contract does not make it happen.

Mutual countervailing actions are also insufficient to revoke a premarital agreement. For example, the spouses' decision to use separate funds to satisfy the mortgage on their marital home does not, in and of itself, terminate the premarital agreement—even if it provides that separate property shall never be used to pay community debt. As a rule, neither oral modifications nor oral revocations are valid.

Texas Family Code Section 4.005 controls amendments and revocations of premarital agreements:

After marriage, a premarital agreement may be amended or revoked only by a written agreement signed by the parties. The amended agreement or the revocation is enforceable without consideration.

Spouses who have been married for years might want to amend, revoke, or replace their old contract with a new agreement. For example, if the economically-dependent spouse will not get a fair benefit upon divorce or probate, this causes strife. The parties may want to amend their premarital agreement. The law controlling the premarital agreement is statutory, that is, amending a premarital agreement after marriage does not transform it into a postnuptial agreement. Those are two different instruments held by two separate bodies of law.

Assuming no divorce or legal separation is pending in Court, the spouses could choose to substitute their premarital agreement entirely with a postmarital understanding. Couples who never had a premarital agreement may want to talk to a family attorney about a postnuptial deal.

POSTMARITAL AGREEMENTS IN TEXAS

In Texas, spouses may enter into a postmarital agreement that covers similar territory as premarital agreements, such as categorizing and dividing property and trusts. They are creating a postmarital agreement (Partition and Exchange Agreement), which is governed by a different part of the Texas Family Code than the premarital agreement. Although similar in some ways, they are also different.

PARTITION AND EXCHANGE AGREEMENT FORMALITIES

First, under Texas Family Code 4.203, a postmarital agreement (Partition and Exchange Agreement) must:

1. be in writing,
2. be signed by the spouses,
3. identify the property being converted,
4. specify that the property is being converted to the spouses' community property, and
5. be enforceable without consideration.

A postmarital agreement might better reflect the spouses' current reality and address areas of continuing conflict. The spouses may now have minor children, work full-time in independent careers, have accumulated substantial assets, and have various business interests.

Circumstances can change throughout a marriage. A postmarital agreement can help spouses keep pace with their lifestyles. Given the most cited reason for divorce is arguments over money, being proactive and reasonably addressing difficult issues with a postmarital agreement may help the couple avoid further matrimonial disputes.

Spouses are free to substitute their premarital agreement with a valid superseding deal, one that provides more equitable terms and covers aspects of marriage that were not anticipated before the wedding.

Postmarital agreements may address many personal financial matters, including:

1. Division of assets and debts in the event of divorce or separation;
2. Provision of spousal support;
3. Contribution to a child's college trust or added support beyond Texas guideline child support;

4. Payment of the family's vacation and travel expenses;
5. Supporting an adult family member with chronic illness or disability;
6. Control of the family business;
7. Inheritance as separate property despite being commingled with marital assets; and
8. Allocating responsibility of specific obligations during the marriage, such as bills or property taxes.

When separated or if a divorce is pending, spouses may no longer be on the same page regarding their premarital or postmarital agreements. These and other serious concerns could be settled through divorce negotiations with a private mediator. Before taking action that may cause regrets later, discuss legal alternatives with a lawyer.

CHAPTER 8
DECLARATORY JUDGEMENTS POST-EXECUTION

SOME LAWYERS TAKE the additional step of obtaining a declaratory judgment after a premarital or postmarital agreement is executed to seek a judicial determination regarding the validity of the agreement. This is done soon after the premarital or postmarital agreement is executed, and before a dispute occurs that would call into question the validity of the agreement.

The reason for asking for a declaratory judgment is based on the premise that under the Texas Civil Practice and Remedies Code 37003(b), a declaratory judgment has the force and effect of a final judgment or decree.

DECLARATORY JUDGMENT ACT SUBJECT MATTER

Chapter 37.004 of the Texas Civil Practice and Remedies Code covers the types of controversies that can be determined by declaratory judgment:

1. A person interested under a deed, will, written contract, or other writings constituting a contract or whose rights, status, or other legal relations are affected by a statute,

municipal ordinance, contract, or franchise may have determined any question of construction or validity arising under the instrument, statute, ordinance, contract, or franchise and obtain a declaration of rights, status, or other legal relations thereunder.

2. A contract may be construed either before or after there has been a breach.

The Uniform Declaratory Judgments Act is a procedural device for deciding cases that are within the Court's jurisdiction, per State v. Morales, 869 S.W.2d 941, 947 (Tex. 1994) and Chambers County v.

TSP Development, Ltd., 63 S.W.3d 835, 840 (Tex. App.-Houston [14th Dist.] 2001, pet. !led). The purpose of the act is to settle and afford relief from uncertainty and insecurity with respect to rights, status, and other legal relations, e.g., Bonham State Bank v. Beadle, 907 S.W.2d 465, 467 (Tex. 1995) and Rush v. Barrios, 56 S.W.3d 88, 105 (Tex. App.-Houston [14th Dist.] 2001, pet. denied) (The purpose of a declaratory judgment is to establish existing rights, status, or other legal relations). The Declaratory Judgments Act is remedial only (Bonham State Bank, 907 S.W.2d at 467).

The Uniform Declaratory Judgments Act does not confer jurisdiction on the trial court, but rather makes available the remedy of a declaratory judgment for a cause of action already within the Court's jurisdiction (Morales, 869 S.W.2d at 947; Rush, 56 S.W.3d at 105). A declaratory judgment is appropriate only if a justiciable controversy exists as to the rights and status of the parties and the controversy will be resolved by the declaration sought, e.g., Bonham State Bank, 907S.W.2d at 467; City of Longview v. Head, 33 S.W.3d 47, 51 (Tex. App.-Tyler 2000, no pet.); and Rush, 56 S.W.3d at 105. A justiciable controversy must be distinguished from an advisory opinion (Head, 33 S.W.3d at 51).

Texas courts do not have the authority to render judgments that merely constitute advisory opinions; see Patterson v. Planned Parenthood of Houston & S.E. Tex., Inc., 971 S.W.2d 439, 443 (Tex. 1998);

Waite v. Waite, 64 S.W.3d 217, 223 (Tex. App.-Houston [14th Dist.] 2001, pet. denied); and Texas Dept. of Public Safety v. Moore, 985 S.W.2d 149, 153 (Tex. App.-Austin 1998, no pet.). An opinion is advisory when the judgment sought would not constitute specific relief to a litigant or affect legal relations; see Continental Cas. Co. v. Texas Bd. of Chiropractic Examiners, 2001 WL 359632 at *2 (Tex. App.-Austin April 12, 2001, no pet.) and Brinkley v. Texas Lottery Comm'n, 986 S.W.2d 764, 767 (Tex. App. Austin 1999, no pet.).The distinctive feature of an advisory opinion is that it decides an abstract question of law without binding the parties, e.g., Continental Cas. Co., 2001 WL 359632 at *2; Brinkley, 986 S.W.2d at 767. Unless there is a justiciable issue, the trial court does not have subject matter jurisdiction under the Texas Declaratory Judgment Act; see J.E.M. v. Fidelity & Cas. Co. of New York, 928 S.W.2d 668, 671 (Tex. App.-Houston [1st Dist.] 1996, no writ). Subject matter jurisdiction refers to the Court's power to hear a particular type of suit, a power that exists by operation of law only and cannot be conferred upon any court by consent or waiver; see Federal Underwriters Exch. v. Pugh, 174 S.W.2d 598, 600 (Tex. 1943).

Lack of subject matter jurisdiction renders a judgment void, rather than merely voidable, so that it may be challenged either directly or collaterally. See Browning v. Placke, 698 S.W.2d 362, 363 (Tex. 1985) (on collateral attack judgment was not shown to have been rendered by a court without jurisdiction); see also Mapco, Inc.

v. Forrest, 795 S.W.2d 700, 703 (Tex. 1990) (an order is void only if the court rendering it had no jurisdiction over the parties, no jurisdiction over the subject matter, no jurisdiction to enter the judgment, or no capacity to act as a court). Errors other than lack of jurisdiction render the judgment merely voidable and must be attacked within prescribed time limits; see Browning, 698 S.W.2d at 363 (Tex. 1985). The distinction between a void and voidable judicial act is: while a void act is entirely null within itself, not binding on either party, and not susceptible to ratification or confirmation, so that its nullity cannot be waived, a voidable act is not absolutely void within itself, but rather is binding until disaffirmed, and may be made finally valid by failure within the proper time to have it annulled, or by subsequent ratification or confirmation; see Brazzel v. Murray, 481 S.W.2d 801, 803 (Tex. 1972) (quoting Murchison v. White, 54 Tex. 78, 81 (1880)). Accordingly, a collateral attack on declaratory judgment affirming the enforceability of a premarital agreement might success- fully allege that no justiciable issue existed at the time the Court entered the judgment (i.e., there was no existing controversy concerning the enforcement of the agreement and thus the issue was not ripe). Further, because no justiciable issue existed, the court rendering the judgment lacked subject matter jurisdiction, and the parties' attempt to bestow such jurisdiction was ineffective. Thus, the declaratory judgment represents, at best, an impermissible advisory opinion.

No reported Texas case discusses the validity of a declaratory judgment affirming the enforceability of a premarital agreement. Cf. Bavido v. Weixel, 459 So. 2d 701 (La. Ct. App. 1984); Eaton v. Eaton, 366 A.2d 121 (Md. Ct. App. 1976); Richardson v. Richardson, 606 N.E.2d 56 (Ill. App. Ct. 1992); Wolfe v. Wolfe, 491 A.2d 281 (Pa. Super. Ct. 1985); Stenson v. Stenson, 359 N.E.2d 787 (Ill. App. Ct. 1977); Kosik v. George, 452 P.2d 560 (Or. 1969); Miller v. Miller, 151 So.2d 869 (Fla. Dist. Ct. App. 1963); and Trossman v. Trossman, 165 N.E.2d 368 (Ill. App. Ct. 1960). Even still, counter-arguments to such an attack may well exist. For example, the Texas Supreme Court has stated that if a court having potential jurisdiction renders a judgment when the potential jurisdiction has not been activated, and the defect is apparent from the face of the judgment, then the judgment is void and subject to either direct or collateral attack; see Fulton v. Finch, 346 S.W.2d 823, 827 (Tex. 1961) (emphasis added). If, however, the Court having potential jurisdiction renders a judgment that contains recitations stating that potential jurisdiction has been activated, then the judgment is voidable, not void, and may be set aside only by a direct attack, as in Akers v. Simpson, 445 S.W.2d 957, 959 (Tex. 1969). The unassailability of the judgment arises because a court of potential jurisdiction has the power to determine whether its jurisdiction has been activated, and the recitations making that determination are immune from attack in a collateral proceeding; see McEwen v. Harrison, 345 S.W.2d 706, 710 (Tex. 1961). Consequently, depending on how the declaratory judgment is drafted, a collateral attack may not be possible. If a collateral attack is not possible, the Texas lawyer also may not have many viable options for direct attack upon a declaratory judgment affirming the enforceability of a premarital agreement. It is unlikely that a direct appeal will still be available, since an appeal must be perfected within 30 days after the judgment was signed, per TEX. R. APP. P. 26.1. However, if the declaratory judgment was signed within the preceding six months, a restricted appeal (formerly an appeal by writ of error) may be available. See TEX. R. APP. P. 30. To bring a restricted appeal, a litigant must demonstrate that (1) he or she is a party to the suit; (2) he or she #led the restricted appeal within six months of judgment; (3) he or she did not participate at trial; and (4) error is apparent on the face of the record. Note that it is very unlikely that a declaratory judgment, entered by consent of the parties, will show error on the face of the record.

Finally, the equitable bill of review may be available. To be successful in a bill of review, the plaintiff must allege and prove: (1) a meritorious defense to the cause of action alleged to support the judgment; (2) which fraud, accident, or the opposing party's wrongful act prevented him from presenting; (3) no fault or negligence of his own; see Baker v. Goldsmith, 582 S.W.2d 404, 406-407 (Tex. 1979). However, a bill of review will not likely correct a declaratory judgment affirming the validity of a marital agreement entered by consent of the parties.

CHAPTER 9
ROLE OF THE FAMILY LAW ATTORNEY

BY NOW, it should be apparent that as beneficial as the prenuptial agreement can be, preparing an enforceable agreement of this nature is not a weekend project for a non-attorney. My recommendation is to hire a lawyer for professional guidance and legal advice during the entire process.

The lawyer you hire will help with the execution of an agreement that serves your interest as the client by meeting your needs and protecting property rights and income from a spousal claim without creating any unnecessary antagonism that might alienate the other party. This will be done through:

1. Negotiation,
2. Information gathering, and
3. The signing of all documents.

Being represented by a lawyer with both drafting and courtroom experience is the best way to make sure the agreement considers:

1. Validity,
2. Voluntariness, and

3. Enforceability.

This will insure the creation of an agreement that will withstand an attack on validity after death or dissolution of marriage.

CONSIDERATIONS FOR CHOOSING A LAWYER

What should you look for when selecting a lawyer to help you with a premarital agreement? A few things to look for include:

1. Practice area
2. Courtroom Experience
3. Personality
4. Communication
5. Accessibility
6. Location
7. Consultation
8. Size of practice
9. Price

PRACTICE AREA

What is the level of the lawyer's knowledge in drafting and negotiating premarital agreements? What type of special knowledge or experience does the lawyer have? My recommendation is not to hire a general practitioner. Look for an attorney who focuses on family or estate law and has experience drafting premarital agreements.

COURTROOM EXPERIENCE

A lawyer's courtroom experience will be significant when drafting premarital agreements to make sure the contract is enforceable. An attorney with this experience will be able to advise a client regarding steps that can be taken to avoid weakness in the contract.

PERSONALITY

Is the lawyer's approach consistent with how you would like to conduct negotiations? Find someone with whom you feel comfortable. Will this attorney focus on your goals as a client? You will be sharing financial and personal information with your attorney, so it is essential to feel comfortable with your lawyer.

COMMUNICATION

You should also consider the method of communication you prefer, such as:

1. Email,
2. Phone,
3. In-person meetings,
4. Texting, or
5. Video conferencing.

Can the attorney you are considering accommodate your preference? How long will it take them to respond to communications with you?

ACCESSIBILITY

Will the lawyer have enough time to devote to your case? How much time will the attorney need to prepare a draft agreement?

LOCATION

How far are you willing to travel to the lawyer's office? Does the attorney charge for their travel time?

CONSULTATION

You should have a consultation with two or three attorneys before deciding who to hire. A consultation should help you better understand the process, what needs to be done, and the attorneys' experience with premarital agreements.

SIZE OF PRACTICE

Will the lawyer handle all aspects of your matter, or will support staff or other lawyers be assisting?

PRICE

There are many factors that can contribute to the price, including:

1. The lawyer's hourly rate
2. The lawyer's experience
3. The comprehensiveness of the agreement
4. Negotiations

CHECKLIST OF THE LAWYER'S ROLE

A lawyer's involvement in the process of negotiation, document review, drafting, and litigating the validity of the agreement is not always understood by clients from the beginning of their representation.

Working with an experienced professional can help you determine what may work best to establish a framework for the negotiations. A lawyer who has worked with many clients will offer advice and options that will help facilitate obtaining a beneficial and enforceable premarital agreement.

If you are concerned about bringing up the idea of a premarital agreement, or if you would like to understand better how they work, meeting with a lawyer will help you understand the nuances and possibilities of premarital agreements.

Premarital agreements can be handled in a beneficial way where legal advice is available and the client's questions are answered before decisions are made and paperwork signed. In many ways, premarital agreements encourage conversations concerning essential matters such as:

1. Married life,
2. Raising a family,
3. Acquiring property, and
4. Future expectations.

INDEPENDENT LEGAL COUNSEL

An attorney can serve as legal counsel during premarital agreement negotiations. Each party should have their attorney to advise on marital rights and information regarding any concerns about the future enforceability of the terms of the agreement.

COMMUNITY PROPERTY

An attorney can explain to a client what their rights would be as to community and separate property with and without a premarital agreement, and what the legal consequences would be in the event of either a divorce or their spouse's death.

Texas is one of nine other states that are under the community property system of law. Therefore premarital agreements typically have sections that cover the topic of how property division will be handled in the event of death and divorce.

The equitable division of assets and debts is essential and should only be made after a discussion with an attorney.

TRANSMUTATION AND COMMINGLING

A lawyer can educate the client on the legal consequences of transmuted and commingled assets. The carefully drafted premarital agreement may provide for future situations where a spouse's handling of their separate property does not result in its being transmuted or commingled with marital assets, although such acts would, in the absence of an agreement, result in the transformation of separate assets into community assets.

Be aware that community property is typically divided 50/50 in most divorces, while only half of the community property is included in the deceased spouse's probate estate.

SPOUSAL MAINTENANCE

A lawyer can explain a party's rights to spousal maintenance in divorce or separation compared to the outcome under specific terms of the premarital agreement. There are important tax considerations associated with the payment and receipt of spousal maintenance. For example, the *Tax Cuts and Jobs Act of 2017* eliminated the alimony deduction in most cases.

LEGAL COSTS AND FEES

A lawyer can discuss option provisions regarding the payment of lawyer fees, court costs, and other expert fees. Who will be responsible for the costs of preparing the premarital agreement? Who will pay costs associated with future litigation concerning the validity of the deal?

CHECKLIST OF THE INITIAL ATTORNEY CONSULTATION

Before meeting with a lawyer to discuss representation, gather information and documentation about the parties' personal finances and upcoming marriage. List both general and specific questions regarding proposed premarital terms of the agreement. At the initial consultation, be ready to:

1. Discuss circumstances
2. Discuss estate planning and probate
3. Discuss alternatives
4. Discuss collaboration

DISCUSS CIRCUMSTANCES

Summarize both parties' premarital circumstances. Ask the potential benefits and detriments of having a premarital agreement, given the events as they are currently known. What financial disclosures are necessary?

DISCUSS ESTATE PLANNING AND PROBATE

Ask about estate planning alternatives to a premarital agreement. What impact will probate have? After marrying, what must be done to integrate each spouse's estate plan with the parties' agreed conditions in the premarital agreement?

DISCUSS ALTERNATIVES

Ask the lawyer to compare and contrast the coverage of a premarital agreement with the range of negotiating or court-ordered temporary orders in a divorce. How do they differ? Although settlement and divorce mediation are strongly encouraged in Texas court proceedings, there is no guarantee that the spouse's plan for separation will resolve all the issues and eliminate the need for a trial.

DISCUSS COLLABORATION

Ask whether the lawyer uses collaborative divorce techniques to help the client negotiate and prepare the premarital agreement. With a collaborative approach, each party is represented by counsel at face-to-face meetings where specific terms and conditions are discussed and arranged. Although one attorney typically takes the lead in drafting the agreement, both lawyers help write up the papers to be signed by the parties. The attorneys usually agree to refrain from representing either spouse in a later divorce or contested probate to foster trust and cooperation.

Premarital agreements can save on the cost of divorce by eliminating the number of issues in contention. Saving money and avoiding protracted court proceedings is possible when a premarital agreement explicitly defines how property and debts are to be allocated.

When a premarital agreement is challenged in probate or divorce, an experienced attorney will be needed to handle the case. If the judge finds that the premarital agreement is not valid, then it may be unenforceable. The party opposing the premarital agreement has the burden of proving that the deal is not valid.

CHAPTER 10
COHABITATION AGREEMENTS

OVER THE PAST SIX MONTHS, I have met with several potential clients who decided to make some major financial decisions with their boyfriend or girlfriend and unfortunately the relationship did not work out.

One lady and her boyfriend had purchased a house and had a child together. Both were named on the deed. In that case, the boyfriend was refusing to help support the child or contribute to any bills related to the house. He was very happy letting his girlfriend support him while he sat at home playing video games. The woman I met with wanted out and wanted to get some orders regarding the child.

In another case a woman again purchased a house with her boyfriend; however, in that case, she was not listed on the deed but had contributed a large amount of money to the house. In this case, he kicked her out of the house and told her not to come back and that she would not see a penny of the money she had paid to the purchase of the house.

In both cases, I hoped that there would be enough evidence to support a claim of common-law marriage. If there was a common-law marriage that would be the easiest way to untangle the couple from each other financially and otherwise. Unfortunately, aside from them having lived together, there was no other evidence. Both women were adamant that they had never intended to be married and had never indicated to anyone that they were married.

This was disappointing because it meant that things would be more complicated and expensive if we were going to be able to help. Her situation is one the reasons divorce exists. However, divorce is not available to unmarried couples.

In the first scenario, we would be able to help get orders in place regarding the child. The woman was also protected because she was on the deed; however, we would have to bring a separate lawsuit regarding that property. In the second scenario, the woman might be out of luck altogether. We would have to dig deeper to see what we could do.

WHAT RIGHTS DO UNMARRIED COUPLES HAVE?

Both women had expected that since they had lived together with their boyfriend that they would be provide with some sort of rights or protection? In short, the answer is no.

This is especially true with respect to property acquired during a relationship. Marital property laws and other family laws were designed to protect married couples and do not apply to unmarried couples. This is true no matter how long the relationship lasted.

Palimony is not a legal concept. Rather, it is a popular term used to describe the division of property or periodic support payments paid to one partner in an unmarried couple relationship by the other partner after the couple breaks up.

The Texas Family Code does not provide for "palimony." This means you cannot gain rights under the Texas Family Code because you lived with someone absent a valid marriage.

CAN AN UNMARRIED COUPLE ESTABLISH RIGHTS AS A COUPLE?

However, it is possible to draft an agreement which might provide for some of the things that could be obtained with a valid marriage.

The Texas Family Code Section 1.08 states:

A promise or agreement made on consideration of marriage or nonmarital conjugal cohabitation is not enforceable unless the promise or agreement or a memorandum of the promise or agreement is in writing and signed by the person obligated by the promise or agreement.

The Texas Business Code allows parties to enter agreements in consideration of "nonmarital conjugal cohabitation." To be enforceable, these contracts or agreements must be:

1. in writing and
2. signed by those who are affected by the agreement.

The Texas Legislature specifically stated that this provision was enacted to curb the number of palimony cases entering the family courts.

Oral agreements will likely not be upheld. At least one court has held that an oral agreement is not enforceable, in Zaremba v. Cilburn.

WHY A COHABITATION AGREEMENT MAY BE A GOOD IDEA

As illustrated in the two examples I gave above, when you are living with someone else and are NOT planning to be married, sometimes lines blur and the couple starts making financial decisions as if they were married.

Then if the relationship does not work out the couple is left with questions regarding who is responsible for any joint debts and who owns the assets. If the couple is not careful someone might be significantly hurt financially.

The problem is partly because the characterization of property acquired by unmarried cohabitants is less clear than that of married couples. Married couples' ownership of property is governed by marital and community property laws.

Under community property laws it does not matter whose name is on the property in most cases; it is still owned by both parties in the marital relationship. This is not true for an unmarried couple.

One solution is a written cohabitation agreement that is signed and meets all the formalities of a regular contract. A cohabitation agreement allows an unmarried couple to legally spell out their rights and obligations toward each other.

Cohabitation agreements can be useful:

1. when one of the parties dies;
2. if the cohabitants decide to end their relationship; and
3. in governing the affairs of the couple while they are living together.

Generally, a cohabitation agreement can be used to:

1. State the couple is not married and should not be considered married;
2. Discuss how expenses are to be paid;
3. Outline who is responsible for what during the living arrangement;
4. Specify who pays the lease or the mortgage;
5. Determine whether the couple will share any financial accounts such as a joint checking account;
6. Identify assets and debts, and who owns them;
7. Specify what property is separate property or jointly owned;
8. Outline how the property will be distributed, should the couple split up; and
9. Establish support payments.

WHAT ABOUT MEDICAL DECISIONS AND ESTATE PLANNING?

Couples also sometimes have concerns regarding estate planning and medical care. Generally, someone who lives with another is not considered an heir under the law and they do not have any rights to make medical decisions the way a legal spouse would.

If this is a concern, then you may want to consider, in addition to a cohabitation agreement, obtaining:

1. estate planning and
2. power of attorney.

DEFENSES TO COHABITATION AGREEMENTS

The defenses to cohabitation agreements are those available under general contract law rather than the limited defenses available against premarital and postmarital agreements under the Family Code.

Common law defenses include:

1. fraud,
2. repudiation,
3. duress,
4. mistake,
5. unconscionability, and
6. ratification.

If you are considering moving in together with your paramour or loved one, then you should think seriously about entering into a cohabitation agreement to protect yourself and eliminate uncertainty regarding your rights and duties to each other. A cohabitation agreement can also provide a measure of security in the event the relationship terminates.

CHAPTER 11

CHECKLIST OF QUESTIONS TO DISCUSS WITH FAMILY LAW ATTORNEY AND YOUR FIANCÉ

MARRIAGE BRINGS financial rights and responsibilities. It is wise to go into marriage understanding these rights and responsibilities. If you are preparing to get married you can make choices about what happens to your property during the marriage, in the case of divorce, or in the event of death. You can make these choices with a premarital agreement.

You and your fiancé will want to make a list of your assets and debts that are currently in each of your names individually. It is required for your premarital agreement, and it is also good to be open and up-front about financial issues with your soon-to-be spouse. Below are some preliminary questions to think about both when preparing to understand how a premarital agreement can be used and before entering into one.

COMMUNITY PROPERTY VS. SEPARATE PROPERTY

1. Will the assets and debts remain separate property, meaning that they will go back to the person who accumulated them before the marriage?

2. Or will your separate property be intermingled with your marital property?
3. What if one person's separate property is used to pay o! the other person's separate debts such as school loans?
4. What if you use separate property to buy a home you will own together?

MARITAL PROPERTY

1. How will you handle the income and assets you accumulate together?
2. Will they be joint and 50/50?
3. Will an alternative arrangement be made?

RESIDENCE

1. Where will you live?
2. What will happen to each residence?
3. How will expenses for the residence be paid?
4. Will you buy a new residence together?
5. If yes, how will the title of the residence be held?
6. What happens to the new residence upon death or divorce?
7. If you are living in a residence owned by your fiancé and purchased before the marriage, will you have the right to remain in the residence upon the owner's death? If so, for how long and how will the carrying costs be paid?

MANAGEMENT OF ASSETS AND INCOME

1. Who will make the financial decisions and handle the checkbook?

2. Will you do it together, or will one person be the primary financial manager?
3. What about large expenditures?
4. Does your spouse need to ask you before buying that plasma TV or designer gown?
5. How will the household bills get paid, and whose responsibility is it to pay them?
6. Do you have similar money styles regarding debt and saving?
7. Have you discussed your long-term financial goals and how each of you will contribute to those goals?
8. If one of you owes spousal maintenance or child support from a prior marriage, how will those payments be made?

RETIREMENT AND SAVINGS

1. What about retirement saving?
2. What will happen to retirement assets and savings acquired prior to and during the marriage?
3. What plans and benefits are available, including survivor benefits?
4. What are government benefits, and will they be received?
5. Is there already an agreement or judgment in place that must be considered?
6. Will you have joint bank accounts, separate bank accounts, or both?
7. Will the decision-making authority be different for premarital property or debt that belonged to one of you before the marriage?

CREDIT AND DEBT

1. Have you seen each other's credit reports? Now might be

a good time to have a serious talk about credit scores and priorities with respect to paying o! old debt or accumulating new debt.

2. Is it likely that either of you might overborrow? Or refuse to borrow, no matter how much sense it makes to the other person?

WORK

1. What are your views on nonmonetary contributions, like raising children or managing the household?
2. What is your expectation about the kinds of jobs and income you will each have?
3. Do either of you anticipate a career change at any point in time?
4. Some jobs are riskier than others, like firefighters, military personnel, and stunt performers. Changing your job can impact the other spouse, especially if you become disabled because of an on-the-job injury.
5. Other jobs pay less but are very personally rewarding. Teachers and nonprofit positions typically don't pay very well. How would you feel if your spouse changed careers?
6. When do you plan to retire? As early as possible, or do you plan to work as long as you're able?
7. Do you anticipate both of you continuing to work after having children? Or would one of you stay home? For how long?
8. How will you handle move-away decisions?
9. What if one of you was transferred for your work and had to move to another state?
10. What if one of you wanted to move closer to extended family after having children?

SPOUSAL MAINTENANCE OR ALIMONY

1. How do you feel about spousal support?
2. Will there be any limitations on the amount, terms, and duration of support?
3. Do you want to make terms about spousal maintenance or alimony that are different than what Texas law allows?
4. Do you both expect to work and to contribute to the household?
5. What are those expectations?
6. Even if you think you are in agreement, it's worthwhile to make sure you're both going into the marriage with the same expectations about earnings and work.
7. Would there be a circumstance that would lead to one partner not working, such as a health problem or the birth of a child? What about going back to school?
8. Does that change how you feel about spousal maintenance or alimony?

GIFTS FROM FAMILIES

1. Sometimes one set of parents or relatives gives a couple a large monetary gift, loan, or home down payment. It is important to make clear what kind of gift this is.
2. Would the gift from the family be marital or community property, or the property of the spouse whose family gave the money?
3. If it's a loan, who would be responsible for repaying it, and how and when?
4. How formal will you be with the documentation if it is a loan?

TAXES

1. Once you are married, your finances will be intertwined for tax purposes unless you agree otherwise as part of your premarital agreement. It is important to be clear on what your attitudes and opinions are regarding paying taxes.
2. Will you !le separate taxes or joint taxes?
3. Does either partner have questionable tax deductions or a lighthearted attitude toward !ling taxes at all? Does that worry the other partner?
4. Is there old tax debt?
5. Who will be responsible for that debt, knowing that a refund while you are married could be seized to pay an old, premarital debt?

HIGHER EDUCATION

1. Sometimes one spouse will want to or need to return to school. This situation may leave one spouse to support the other while he or she pursues a degree. In this situation, it is important to communicate clearly the expectations of each party.
2. Will one of you be attending college, graduate school, or professional school during the marriage?
3. Will one of you have to support the other while he or she is in school?
4. How will student loans be repaid?
5. Would the expectations about income and earnings change if one person wants to go back to school after you've been married several years?

DURATION OF PREMARITAL AGREEMENT

1. It is up to you and your spouse to decide how long a premarital agreement may remain in effect. Couples can ask themselves if the agreement will stand forever or if it will expire at some point.
2. Does having children change your opinion on how your agreement should work?
3. What about being married 10 years, 20, 30, or 50 years? Would the agreement ever expire or be renegotiated?
4. If you separate, does it matter who chooses to end the marriage? Does it matter why?
5. Would you want for the agreement to be renegotiated at a specific time, like five years after the marriage, or after the birth of the first child?

BUSINESS OWNERSHIP

1. Is there an interest in a business?
2. If yes, does the business generate income?
3. How is the income dispersed?
4. Are there liabilities associated with the business?
5. Does the business own real property?
6. You or your spouse own a business separately, there are special issues you should consider: Would your prenuptial agreement include an indemnification on the business debts and taxes—business, personal, back taxes, payroll taxes?
7. Are there issues with the type of business entity, like a subchapter S corporation or d/b/a, and how the corporate spouse determines his or her own income?
8. Many small corporations have a lot of discretion as to

how much of the corporation's income is taken as salary or income for the corporation's officers or employees.

9. Do you want to make provisions for forensic accounting or auditing books in the event of a separation or divorce?
10. Do you want an agreement on how much income will be contributed to the household and how much might be kept separate?
11. What if a premarital business generates a new business or subsidiary after the marriage?
12. What if one or the other of you works for the other person in a pre-marital business? There can be many "out of job market" issues, so negotiating your terms of employment with your spouse before joining the business can be an important step.

HEALTH CARE COVERAGE

1. What is the current health care coverage, and will there be any changes?
2. Is there long-term care insurance in place?

FAULT

1. Fault can be defined as who is to blame for the divorce. Fault can be evidenced by an affair or drug or alcohol abuse, among other things. However, most state laws either won't consider fault, or barely consider fault, in dividing property or awarding spousal support in a divorce.
2. How do you and your fiancé feel about fault?
3. Would it make a difference to you in your property settlement or spousal support if you felt one person

contributed more to the breakdown of the marriage than the other person?

DEATH OR DISABILITY

1. You will want to have a comprehensive estate plan in place soon after your wedding, particularly if you have children from previous relationships, so that your assets and debts are handled the way you intend if you were to pass away.
2. Does it make a difference if you're separated or living separately when one of you dies (even though you haven't "led for a divorce) or if one of you dies while you're happily married?
3. Do either of you have children already, or people who'd inherit from you?
4. Do you have life insurance?
5. Who will you name as beneficiary on your retirement plans, IRAs, and survivor annuity benefits on pension plans?
6. Would your prenuptial agreement end at death?
7. Will the surviving spouse be able to support the same lifestyle in the event of your death?
8. Are there certain family heirlooms or money which you'd like to make sure end up with one person's family?
9. What would happen if one of you became incapacitated or disabled?

ESTATE PLANNING

1. What estate planning documents are currently in place?
2. What estate planning needs to be done to reflect future goals?

3. What are the current beneficiary designations on assets, and do they need to be changed or reaffirmed?
4. Will there be a waiver of the spouse's rights to the other's estate, or will both spouses choose not to waive their rights?

GENERAL

To begin drafting a premarital agreement, you will each need a complete list of your current assets, debts, and income, as well as any health issues you might have.

You may also want to consider including a clause that says you will mediate any issues that come up that you can't resolve on your own or that you will seek professional marriage counseling before considering divorce. Also, another helpful clause may state that the two of you will choose to mediate in the event of a divorce, or use a collaborative law or alternative dispute resolution process rather than litigation.

CHAPTER 12
CONCLUSION

I HOPE this book has shown you that a premarital agreement or postmarital agreement is an opportunity to begin or continue a marriage with a clear sense of each other's values and priorities.

Discussing and working on a premarital agreement can also help establish the direction you and your spouse would like to take your

financial relationship. When the process is handled well, it involves the exchange of knowledge and a discussion of how your decisions will impact your marriage. The process involves establishing communication, listening, and recognizing the emotions and concerns of your spouse or future spouse.

It is important to approach the process with the goal of setting a foundation for trust, your goals, and your spouse or future spouse's goals.

If you still have questions after reading this book and you need a personalized plan and answers regarding your situation, you can accomplish this by contacting an attorney at our law !rm.

CHAPTER 13
TAKING THE NEXT STEP

A PREMARITAL AGREEMENT can be tailored individually to suit any couple's needs or situation. If desired, a "sunset" clause may be included, which specifies the date that the entire prenuptial agreement will expire and no longer have any binding effect on either party.

When establishing a prenup, the agreement must be in writing, signed by both parties, and include full disclosure of both parties' assets and liabilities. In addition, each party is required to retain their own lawyer to separately represent their individual interests. A Family Court judge must then evaluate the prenuptial agreement as of the date of its signing to ensure that rules for establishing the prenup have been followed.

WE ARE HERE FOR YOU

If you are engaged to be married, it is essential to know all of your legal options. Whether you are just thinking about establishing a premarital agreement or are ready to move forward with the process, our highly regarded Texas family law attorneys at the Law Office of

Bryan Fagan PLLC are here to safeguard your assets and secure your future.

Your peace of mind is essential. Please contact us 832-219-6692 if you would like to schedule a free, confidential consultation.

Experience the Law Office of Bryan Fagan PLLC Difference

CHAPTER 14

DO NOT MAKE THIS DECISION BY YOURSELF!

I HOPE this book has given you a better understanding of what to expect and how to protect your right to fair treatment. I hope you have been introduced to enough concepts and legal principles to picture your future and how to begin navigating toward success. Thank you for investing your time with me.

I'd like to return the favor and offer you something in kind. Normally, I charge clients $500.00 n hour for my time. However, if you call my office and mention that you've read this book, I would be happy to waive that charge and provide an initial consultation for free.

If you have experienced uncertainty, sadness, and frustration. Allow me to help restore your peace of mind. Knowledge is power. With my help, you can gain the knowledge to take back control and shape the future you deserve.

Please call my team now at (832) 219-6692 to schedule your consultation. I am looking forward to helping you put the past behind you and enjoy a brighter and more hopeful future.

Take action today toward
YOUR NEW FUTURE!

FREE CONSULTATION
($500 value)

Call:
832-219-6692
or visit:
www.bryanfagan.com

CHAPTER 15

THE MOST INCREDIBLE FREE GIFT EVER

Learn How to Claim a Free Copy of My First Book,
The Texas Divorce Handbook

FREE GIFT

Call our office today:
832-219-6692

or visit:
https://www.bryanfagan.com/resources/

ABOUT THE AUTHOR

Attorney Bryan J. Fagan, of the Law Offices of Bryan Fagan, has spent most of his law career specializing in family law. He is a certified member of the College of the State Bar of Texas, which is an honorary society established in 1982 by the Supreme Court of Texas. In his online posts and books, he succeeds in taking the complex language of the law and making it understandable to the general public. *25 Dirty Tricks to Guard Against and How to Counter Them* is Bryan's second book. *The Texas Divorce Handbook, Volume One* was published in 2017.

Made in the USA
Monee, IL
04 November 2026

67384913R00056